THE LOST COUNTRY OF SIGHT

ANHINGA PRESS

THE LOST COUNTRY OF SIGHT

NEIL AITKEN

2007 PHILIP LEVINE PRIZE FOR POETRY

SELECTED BY C. G. HANZLICEK

ANHINGA PRESS
TALLAHASSEE, FLORIDA 2008

Cover art: *Man Entering the Waves*, digital painting by C. L. Knight
    (based on a photograph of his father by Neil Aitken)
Author photograph: Dawnae Wilson
Cover design, book design, and production: C. L. Knight
Typesetting: Dean Newman
Type Styles: titles set in Poppl and text set in Adobe Jensen Pro

Library of Congress Cataloging-in-Publication Data
The Lost Country Of Sight by Neil Aitken – First Edition
ISBN – 978-1-934695-06-7
Library of Congress Cataloging Card Number – 2008931767

This publication is sponsored in part by a grant
from the Florida Department of State,
Division of Cultural Affairs, and the Florida Arts Council.

Anhinga Press Inc. is a nonprofit corporation dedicated wholly to the
publication and appreciation of fine poetry and other literary genres.

For personal orders, catalogs
and information write to:
Anhinga Press
P.O. Box 10595
Tallahassee, Florida 32302
Web site: www.anhinga.org
E-mail: info@anhinga.org

Published in the United States
by Anhinga Press
Tallahassee, Florida
First Edition, 2008

For my father

ABOUT THE COVER

"Man Entering the Waves" by C.L. Knight

The painting on the cover is based on a photograph of the wreck of the Peter Iredale on the coast of Astoria, Oregon by Neil Aitken. The figure walking out toward the sea is his father — who moved into the camera's line of sight at the moment the photo was taken.

CONTENTS

ix   Acknowledgments

I

5   In the Long Dream of Exile
6   Outside Plato's Republic, the Last Poets Wait for Departure
8   Leaving the Plane
9   Four Hours to Taipei
10   Ghost Passport
11   In Hsin Chu
12   The Art of Forgetting
13   Cycling in the Dark
14   Postcard from Taipei
15   Gift

II

19   Letter from Home
20   Burials
21   Losing the Hawk
22   Planting Tulips
23   Forgetting to Fill Up in Saskatoon
24   Seeking Shelter at -50°
25   At the End of Poetry
26   My Father as Landscape
27   Halfway
28   How We Are Saved

III

31   Counting Winters in Los Angeles
32   To Jeremiah, Dreaming
34   Litany
36   Hermit
37   To the Street Musician

38   All the Names of Children and Homes We May Never Know

39   Homecoming

41   Here and There

42   Considering Photography

43   For the Drowned

44   The Memory Theatre

45   Water Epigraph

47   The Mortician's Bookkeeper

48   For Sal Paradise, Lost in America

49   Man Pulled from the Earth (El Salvador)

    IV

55   In the Country I Call Home

56   How the World Fits Together

57   After Neruda

59   What I Know About Abstraction

60   The Center of Memory

61   Elegy for Grey

62   Traveling Through the Prairies, I Think of My Father's Voice

63   Kite Flying

64   Credo

65   Kundiman

66   The Art of Memory

67   My Father, Waking to Work

68   First Poem

69   An Hour Before Arriving, I See Home

70   The Shape of Things

71   Prodigal

72   I Dream My Father on the Shore

75   Notes

78   About the Author

ACKNOWLEDGMENTS

I am grateful to the editors of the following publications, in which these poems, sometimes in slightly different versions, first appeared: *Avatar Review, Barn Owl Review, Beyond the Valley of Contemporary Poets, Concelebratory Shoehorn Review, Crab Orchard Review, The Drunken Boat, Inscape, Locus Point, MiPOesias, Pebble Lake Review, Poetic Diversity, Portland Review, Prairie Poetry, Quill & Parchment, RHINO, Rock & Sling, Silk Road, Sou'wester, Spillway,* and *Stirring.*

Special thanks to friends and mentors Chris Abani, Christopher Buckley, Juan Felipe Herrera, Lance Larsen, Leslie Norris, and Maurya Simon, for their critical insight and abundant encouragement. Thank you to my many friends in the Creative Writing Program at the University of California, Riverside, as well as the Idyllwild Summer Poetry Program and the writing community at Kundiman. For their valuable comments and close readings of this manuscript in its various incarnations, I am especially grateful to Ching-In Chen, Frankie Drayus, Yuzun Kang, Nancy Lambert, Heather Long, Chi Lam, and R.A. Villaneuva. Thank you as well to the faculty and students of Cal State Fresno, C.G. Hanzlicek for selecting this book, and to Lynne Knight and Rick Campbell at Anhinga Press for bringing this book into its final form. Most of all, I wish to thank my father, Kenneth Aitken for leaving me with a love of language and history; my mother, Christine Mei-Chiang Aitken, for keeping culture and family traditions alive; and, my sister for teaching me the true measure of friendship.

THE LOST COUNTRY OF SIGHT

In the disappearance of small things, I read the tokens of my own dislocation, of my own transiency. An exile reads change the way he reads time, memory, self, love, fear, beauty: in the key of loss.
— André Achiman, *Letters of Transit*

Because of the way a name, any name,
Is empty. And not empty. And almost enough.
— Larry Levis, "Those Graves in Rome"

I

IN THE LONG DREAM OF EXILE

You are counting the dark exit of crows
in the rear view mirror, or from the top of an overpass
looking back into the last flames of cloud.
Your car, steel to the world of flint, rests listless
with its windows wide, the stars slipping in
and settling down for the night.

Now, what you could not leave rides in boxes
heavy with numbers and places you've already
turned into poems. There is nothing left
in your pockets, your clothes worn down
to this list of miles taking you out of the known earth.

Outside your open window, the dark repeats
like the wind in late fall, twisting the names
of familiar back roads into a long rope of sighs.
You could lower yourself down with such longing.
It could be a woman or a young girl, the way the light
clings to that body like a sheet of immaculate heat,
invisible to the eye, but something, you are certain,
something that must be on the verge of love.

OUTSIDE PLATO'S REPUBLIC,
THE LAST POETS WAIT FOR DEPARTURE
Hong Kong International Airport, 1989

... the poet himself is a China
        — Liu Hongbin, Chinese poet-in-exile

1.

This one, tired from the long journey,
leans back in his airport chair. The stain of travel,
tattoo of sweat and the lips of sleeping women
pressed unknowingly to his shoulders mid-flight.
How their faces turned inward the way
a cat's pink tongue fills a wound
with an instinct for sweetness and iron.
Grounded, he is a castoff map, a blankness
scarcely smudged by the sounding rings
of impinging continents. Land he has only seen
through mists. Has only witnessed in the fine print
at the bottom of passports and visas, the insides of cans,
the raised edges of boxes made somewhere else.
Somewhere forgettable where the sick and insane
piece each plastic toy together, immune to pleasure.

2.

In the corner, against the bullet-proof glass,
another raises his arms high above his head,
as if in prayer, or uttering a name to be nailed
like a piton into a hardened cliff face. This unbending
yearning. These barren limbs sprouting from a man
worn smooth by wind and water. How they stretch,
reaching for a heaven of silence, some dim realm
of rope and boards. A bridge. A strict metered offering.
Even. Still. The emptiness of fired clay. A scale.
A measure of wanting. Each hand a receptacle for ghosts.

3.

The last one traces the outbound curve
of an O that returns to its origin again,
stopping once before moving on. She thinks
of round coins punched through with squares,
the angle of characters lifted in relief, the thin
red string that holds them together around her neck.
O, she opens her mouth in a question wide enough
to hold a world the shape of her lips. O is the letter
she leaves at the gate for her lover, for the one
who is always nowhere, too late and too soon.

LEAVING THE PLANE

Kaohsiung International Airport, 1993

To the left through the gap
where the corridor meets the side of the plane,
I glimpse the darkening sky and a lateness
which could be smog or a low mist
blurring what might be mountains into rain.

Everything feels strange
and yet familiar. I remain confused by the weather,
the blare of traffic beyond the gates, and all these voices
surrounding me in a language I once knew as a child.

Standing outside the terminal waiting for my ride,
I want to go back in time — tell my younger self
to keep something, anything, words to describe the heat
or the dark unsettling weight of home and regret.

FOUR HOURS TO TAIPEI

Emptied of thought,
my head against the grey
window of the car.

In what should be dark, but isn't,
the constant barrage of light flares up
from waterstained apartment buildings
and rundown homes on the hills, or gleams
at the side of the road, and every point
in between. Plastic store signs
lit from within, everywhere.
Scooters and taxis disappear,
leaving only the last trace of their tail lights,
        like fireflies escaping into the night.

The road hums like a tired monk
at the end of a Buddhist wake
long after the body has drifted
into the river of stars.

GHOST PASSPORT

When I wake to the city I once called home
and now return to, I wake stranger and son,
at once present and longing. Almost wordless
except for a name bestowed by a grandfather
over-fond of fortunes and women. I keep
a half dozen numbers, insufficient to count
even my finger tips, let alone my years.
Even my hand is distant, a cipher that defies
ready description. My body an unknown quantity,
a strange transcription of limbs. Until at last,
I am merely a ghost among the living, wandering
deep in the endless rising grey of buildings,
new and empty. Vacant. Lost among the streets
that fold into each other, like creases in the skin
where arms bend, where the mouth opens wide
to take in food, the only ambassador I recall.

IN HSIN CHU

Stronger than gravity, the wind
is a constant gale, or so it seems
in late summer and early fall
when not only paper and leaves,
but street signs rattle and strain
against hot air, and small children
in light weight clothes
almost ascend into the sky
like stars blown free
from the city's bright web of lights.

What is invisible makes itself
manifest in miracles, letters from home
disappear only to surface again
plastered against a chain link fence
two towns away. Rain moves horizontally
as if writing itself into the wind,
a palimpsest of salt and storm,
the coding of factories and sweat.

What messages it brings,
I cannot read or comprehend.
My shirts yellowed with sun and iron water,
their own unraveling codex of love
and loss, and the secret names
of post office faces I can't recall from graves.

I lean back into it and bike slowly,
trying to travel in a straight line
as if I were light, or merely its memory,
passing through the dark.

THE ART OF FORGETTING

How to swim, how to ride a bike — even how to voice
my own name in my mother's tongue, each sound
a hard and pitted salt plum I marry to my teeth,
but cannot break open.

Forgetting is in the blood, something gleaned
from my grandmother — her hate strong enough
to wipe clean the first two years of married life,
the loss of her world, my mother's birth.

When I wake this morning to the cloud-dim Taipei sky
and dress in that early light that filters in somehow
through a hundred shades of smog, it is hard to believe
it has been a year already in this home not quite home.

Here, at the gate of memory, I am not my grandmother
grown transparent with age, but rather some lost son come
in stranger's clothes, the air ripe with incense and ash.
I want to remember this year and the one yet to be.

They say that the muscles have memory, that the body recalls
any motion rehearsed over time. An old horse always returns.
Mile after mile, my body relearns Taiwan the hard way — I feel it
when I move, in the way my calves have hardened, in the scar

on my chest where my muscles split wide when a truck door opened
in front of my bike, in the callouses on my knees where I have knelt
every morning on the cement and tile floors and offered a prayer
full of fire and forgetting for someone come down to loosen my tongue,

to unlock that rusted door and let what beats within go free.

CYCLING IN THE DARK

I sing low and under my breath,
these hymns, these words full of longing,
not for anyone else, not even for God,
but for me. For something to hold on to.
Even in movement, there is a hush that builds
with this prayer against falling.

Here, in that close space occupied only by me
and the bicycle and the distant white shirt
of the one ahead of me, I find a certain peace,
a place outside of language.

My feet move in a steady rhythm,
circle after circle. The tires roll forward
over the pavement, the trash, the blood-like stains
of *binglan* spit out on the streets. I ignore
the man pissing against the wall in the shadows,
the sharp scent of his urine blending
with the open sewers that run the edge of the road.

What I can't ignore is absence. When I look up
into the night sky, blank and amnesiac,
there is no trace of satellites, only grey upon grey,
smog upon cloud, no memory of stars.

POSTCARD FROM TAIPEI

In the absence of a train, I wait for the distant hum
of the rails. The slow sun's return. Even a voice
to name another voice. Everything dim, I search
the city's haze for a discernible line. For something
that moves. For anything to hold.

The names of Buddha, ink brush on rain polished steps.
Betelnut and blood. The yellow-robed monks sleeping.
All morning this silence. This pervasive stay of the world.
The walls are still. The clouds are forming pearls.

Lost luggage, twice-bound with twine and ribbon,
contents unknown, sits to my side anxious for reunion.
For something akin to what we want from longing.
What we dream mid-journey in the silence of cars.
The rattle of steel frames. The substance of sleep.

The tin roofs sounding in the wind.
What I recall of beauty.

GIFT

There is always cold at my heels, the tall ships
of thunder, small men with seeds. This is my gift.
This storm I bequeath to the acres of graves,
the bent necks of reeds, trees I remember.
More than color, I leave rain on doorsteps.
Deep into night. I drown the dust-heavy barns.
Make red the dulled wood. Carry the dry-veined leaves
of maples back into streets stained with earth and tires,
black as hard coffee. I am always heavy with grey,
its sharp scent of longing. The taste of uncanceled stamps.
Borneo. Hong Kong. Nicaragua. Belize. A passage of water.
I return your sorrows unsigned. I am unhinged. I am a man
with a bag half-full of teeth. An echo of iris. Blood print of cobalt.
All night, I am weaving this filigree of darkness. All night
a net of rivers blooms. Someone is singing a love song for water.
Someone is digging a grave for the moon.

If I stop, I might see her — some white-haired goddess
of winter and mist, trailing behind me through the high-walled streets.
One hand cool on my shoulder, another pressed through the back
to iceberg skin. Already I know, she will not ask for time,
for black-inked names, only some token of trust, a miracle of geese.
For anything bent on returning.

LETTER FROM HOME

My father's words
laid down
like old shoes
at a back door.

Worn out, grey,
or that distant pale
that night paints the world
just before dawn.

Not knowing
how far this road goes on
moving in slow circles
or sinking into crisp unfathomed snow.

My father sleeping
in long sighs, unaware
of the way a line disappears
at the edge of meaning.

How few words he takes
to recreate a world
in the mind of a son
longing for home.

The last remnants of trees
pulled from the earth
stay hidden for years
till the wind blows them free.

BURIALS

Pulling through Montana in the snow
we cling to the tail lights of the last car
blurring back into the darkness.

"Like the inside of a coffin," my father says,
as if knowing the exact shade the dead see,
lying stiff, frozen eyes peering up through closed lids —

he shifts in his seat, watches the road disappear,
thinks again of dying and the burials we've seen,
his father's simple reduction to ashes.

How small the urn, how light, for a man
that stood 6' 3", carried a boy on his shoulders,
lived on trains as a youth, picked apples as a man.

This past summer, watching him thin
to disappearing, blurring out lines between lives,
my father trying to return pieces, fragments, time,

the body burning, the dark smells of crematoriums,
funeral homes, and pale faced lawyers.
Something merges, ends, and begins.

My father placing the ashes back into the air,
offerings to the skies, to the seas,
unaware how Buddhist he is at this moment,

how the faint sound of bagpipes echoes,
how the ashes fall catching light,
reflecting something back into the silence,

the dark birth of the sun coming into view.

LOSING THE HAWK

I am like a gull lost between heaven and earth
— Tu Fu

My father says nothing for miles,
watching an invisible speck in the sky,
a single hawk circling far above our car's silent passage
through fields of dust and grain.

No prey to be seen,
and no prayer but the wind
pushing one way, then another
through the cracked windows of the old car.
The world outside as empty as a beggar's palm.

At dusk, we rest at the side of the road
in the middle of nowhere and stare up
at the sky, now filling with stars and wanderers,
ignorant of the names and lines which connect them,
caught in the slow sway of the Northern Lights.

Beyond our view, geese call from a cage of willows
set at the water's edge, and the old river moves unseen
through the tall heads of grain. We lose the hawk
in the darkness — hear only wings overhead,
their wordless lullaby ascending into night.

PLANTING TULIPS

Before my father dies
I should like to dig once more
in the back garden behind the old home
where I spent so many summers,
striking a rhythm with dirt clods breaking
against a shovel's blade, pressed firmly to the earth.

Should like to cradle each bulb in my stained hands,
as if to bless it before burial, or to peer into its opaque skin,
wondering at the rough beauty of unseen roots,

then tamp down a small mound and pray for rain
and wait for the slow green signs of birth.

FORGETTING TO FILL UP IN SASKATOON

We ran on empty for an hour,
three boys in a borrowed car,
miles away from anywhere
but these dead farm towns
without street lamps or oil.

Just burnt out gas stations
and the low moans of cattle
shifting in the dark.

Dry as December, we coasted
all the way home, whispering prayers
and holding our breath as if to lighten
the load till the faint lines of the city
rose at the edge of our view,
like the far off fires of a familiar shore,
and we pulled ourselves in —
weary men, tired of the sea.

SEEKING SHELTER AT -50°

Trying to thaw,
we sat by the dim warmth
of the wood burning stove.
Brittle as our clothes, frozen.
Our few words — a visible fog.

Outside the thin wooden walls,
the wind-driven branches tapped
like blind men or perhaps
a prisoner in solitary
testing the depth of his world.

Down the north gravel road,
an abandoned farmhouse
full of imagined lights, whispers,
the shuffling of raccoons,
old papers.

In the gullies, ghost cars
still shining like new
rested where they were thrown
miles from anywhere.

And far above, stars
the color of snow — each
a lone boat drifting
in the dark sea.

AT THE END OF POETRY

First, the high brilliant sky in its perfect cold,
the snow laid down in drifts as thin
as flame, and the last taste of barbed wire
rusting on the post, almost gone.

From the memory of one thing
comes another, grief embodied
in a scarf whipped free by the wind,
the red-tailed hawk spun in the distant sun,
the smallest of satellites, the frozen earth
complete with tiny lakes of glass.

Here, almost invisible against the deafening fields,
the remains of a small boat sunk low
in the drained slough, forgotten
but for the crows and the few final reeds
that persist in its shade.

These are journeys we never take,
but fold back over again, clippings of fires,
wars, deaths, rebirths. At night, the coals
settle in the stove, the kettle steams.

Outside, always a man in a heavy coat
with a lantern in hand moving through the dark
toward the whitening ghosts of trees.

MY FATHER AS LANDSCAPE

My father is a forest in winter where death
has cast her grey nets wide over the outstretched limbs.
He is not the pale skin of snow, nor what lies beneath:
last year's leaves pooling in remembered red, the tumbled nests
of wrens, the bones of sparrows lightened by sorrow, whatever
the winds have laid down in their paths. He is the bear who lingers
at the edge of the frozen creek though the blackberries are gone.
He is the tree split by a summer storm, the last of the pollen
caught in an awkward breeze. The deer stepping back out of the light.

But I am not a forest. I am a road cutting through its midst.
I am what the mountain yields, the path through tall shadows
of pines and maples. I am the line that stitches the earth, my body
an unending arc of stone and gravel. I am the eye, the sight, the sign
at the edge of a ravine before the drop to nothing. I am the steel rail
on which you lean, the cross, and the wild flower burning against the dark.

HALFWAY

It has been hours now. The sun long swallowed in a growing
bank of grey. Your body turned machine. The noiseless circle
of arms and feet and their thousand-fold revolutions. How many hours
have you pushed on, parting the cold waves anticipating that last stroke
forward, the one that ends in the earth, a foot in the weeds, or a voice
in the ear calling you free? How long till the water holds you fast
and claims you her own? And what now, what to do with the night sky
so full of nameless want and need?

HOW WE ARE SAVED

Gathered at the side of my father's bed, his body still
warm to the touch, his eyes darkening like those of a fish
laid high on the river bank, the sun slipping through
half-closed blinds into the cream-colored room —
we have come to dress him one last time.

To bend his arms, not for prayer, but to slide the sleeves
of the clean white shirt over, to pull each limb through —
pants, socks, shoes — till the body is clothed, readied at last
to meet whatever fiery light will embrace it first. The kiln,
the grave, love's small white cloud that arrives just before rain.

No, this is just a body. Clay and water. Hollow. What we shed
in the white room over words of prayer. What we weave of memory,
grace for grace, this already faded circle of thought and longing.
Oh, this body — grown more wind than flesh, even as the air leaves
his lungs, there is a knocking at the door, something dark
and hopeful rising to my lips, the strains of a very old song.

COUNTING WINTERS IN LOS ANGELES

I no longer mark what falls in passing,
iron stones blazing through the night sky,
leaves turning dry in the autumn breeze,
or old men curled around fires
watching yesterday's news offered up
as ashes to the dark.

Hiding in the concrete-celled city,
my head is full of another country's snow,
a loose wind blowing through my room
at night, when I cannot sleep
and lie to myself in dreams
I've committed to memory.

I am a stranger to the city that burns
with too much neon. Each night
I wind my sun-burnt car
through towers of glass and steel,
listen to the radiant hum of static,
the muted signal of an invisible sun,
the slow ticking questions keeping time.

What winter will take me home
down an ice-covered road
past the grey boarded shacks,
beyond the bending river's spine,
then plant me low
beneath the white-haired trees?

What wind will wrap itself
around my waist, and lower me down
to sleep and distant rain?

TO JEREMIAH, DREAMING

You wake on fire
with an arm touched by God
or his angels, only to find
the world outside the same
sudden dark you lost
years ago.

Every night is the same.

The moon in its phases
falls across the opened pages
of unread books,
draws a cipher of light
in your empty cell.

You roll from your bed
startled by the sound
of men fighting in the street,

stirred
at the precise moment
when the lights fail in the city.

You glimpse the world

and wonder:

how each gift of coal
burns your lips,

how cool
flesh is
when unburdened of a soul,

how this hollow place
in your stomach always turns,
growing one blood word
at a time, like a child wanted
and yet unknown.

LITANY

For Raphael Alberti

angel of postage stamps
and unknown addresses
feet black with ink

watermark angel
with paper-thin wings
angel of letters and canvas
angel of resignation

angel of dust bins
storm clouds
unsifted wheat
tide-driven angel of sandbars

broken winged angel
of crows and magpies
angel of dark-eyed women
who taste of the sea

angel of scissors
metal-bound angel of dreams
stone-lipped angel of memory

angel of forgetting
of blood-iron
and smoke

unknown angel of agony
small twisting angel of grief
wooden angel
blind angel of angles
crossbeams
knotted rope

the one here
hovering
over my desk
as I write
the angel of weight
red dwarf stars
and mercy

outside my window
the angel of machinery
turning in the earth,
green and gold and red
a clockwork divinity

Come, come

HERMIT

How the world is full of silence
you say to yourself, closing the door
behind you as you slip back into your cell
like a ghost or a letter returned unopened,
its words unweighed, unknown. A cloud
before rain, before storm. A bottled wish
in a sea of grey with nowhere to go.

You stand next to the gas stove
listening to the steady *click-click*
of sparks in the empty space
trying to set the invisible
aflame. And when it catches fire at last,
you watch it rush outward as if mad,
driven by a hunger for air, for something
to say to the dark and metallic world.

TO THE STREET MUSICIAN

What rattles at the bottom of the voice
raised against the cold is not a question of grace,
nor an echo of storms burning in a street lamp's glare.

Some nights, all you have are fingers
and old wood
blending steel and voice
down an electric line to the heart,

How you hold this six-stringed mystery close to your chest,
unlock hands from neck, let the hollow frame fill,
an old vessel of words burning slowly down.

All night you travel in the ears
of women in empty cars passing
in the dark, wondering to themselves:

How far is it to home? How far to the narrow bed,
the open window, the quartered moon sinking
                    like a hand across the fretted sky?

ALL THE NAMES OF CHILDREN
AND HOMES WE MAY NEVER KNOW

In her blue-skinned letter, folded in thirds,
she wants to know why the world unfolds
in a way that leaves us on opposite coasts
stuttering in inked pages and uncertain hope,
with the wide back of America between us.
And though she tells me of her brother
born again upstate, in this time for robbery,
and her father found, thought dead for years,
now living outside their old village by the Mekong
with a new wife and six kids — I want only to hold her
closer than this, to wonder at her anger and awe
that burn like a brand against the skin. *Give it time,*
I want to whisper in the ear of the one I might love.
Even the bamboo has forgotten the napalm at last.
Each arch of a word on the page is only a small temple,
or perhaps, a makeshift boat of plank and reed
in an endless surge of ink. Held against the light,
I want to believe some trace of her fingers remains
caught between these lines. Something I can gather
like stones from a river, whatever love carries
in its small unyielding tides, the earth breaking wide
from the moon. The trees bent at the water's edge.

HOMECOMING

There is a song at the beginning of every journey,
though I keep this to myself,

listening instead for the sound of each soul passing,
their frustrated voices swelling in chorus,

clock hands heavy and circling
while we stay in our places, waiting for the steel swans to fly.

The earth rotates another degree.

As Odysseus,
I slowly make my way home:
Burbank to Vancouver,
by way of San Francisco and Seattle.

Moving port to port,
stranded,
meeting strangers,
pastors,
programmers,
land developers,
lotus eaters.

Homecoming through metal and glass:
the man-faced woman at customs
laughs with clenched teeth
when I tell her

I have nothing to declare.

Long hours fighting sleep,

no one to greet me,
fog, snow, rain,
wind moving through tunnels.

The song at the beginning —
still listening for souls.

HERE AND THERE

There's always an echo in the telling — something that remains
hidden in the hand that passes over the sky. And now I can see it,
if only through her eyes for this moment. That sky scraped wide
over Joshua Tree in the dark, and the stars ringing like a chord of light
struck from the depths of some irreconcilable blue. Sudden or slow.
I do not ask why her hair is almost gone, why her body is now so frail,
as if grown over an architecture of dust, that common remnant of longing.
  God, she says, *it was beautiful ...*
          What could she tell me,
beyond the desert, its dreams of salt and storm?
Here is a tree, a spent fist of flames, she seems to say, standing in the shadows.
Here is the wind. The freeways are filling with strangers.
The sun is coming down. *Here is the road*
       we drove all night to find a way home.

And when I leave, there are men at every corner lighting my way.
Each selling oranges, offering with their hands the bitter
and the sweet, until they blend like a river of lamps, burning.

CONSIDERING PHOTOGRAPHY
Astoria, Oregon

Outside Astoria in a borrowed car, I drive the long road
up the coast, past blackened timbers rising
from old wharves consumed by the sea. A mystery of wood.
A canticle of wind sung at the fencepost by the crows.

Even if I try, the brochures bent double tell me nothing
of the grave-heavy shore, speak only of the great
rusted frames of ships with Norwegian names. Holes
in their sides where the wind sounds, and a man can walk out
to the sea perfectly framed. The shutter closes.

The Finns who built this place now sink back into their beds,
drown their rats in beer, their sorrow in the storms their fathers
knew by name. Now their fathers sleep instead, buried with the fish
they hauled onto blood-ready decks. Ghosts all,
even the fish are gone.

Absent the gulls, only a white crust of salt, a smooth piece
of rose-colored glass reflecting sun, the image of man
is more like an eye turned to a small hole in the sky,
the corner of a billboard peeling free, or a lighthouse
raised on the edge of the known world.

Lewis and Clark saw none of this when they waded in,
moccasins wet, and worn from too many miles. They fell down,
sick and weak, turned down the fire, watched the stars drown
one by one in the open sea.

When I pull into the next town,
even the buildings have turned grey.

FOR THE DROWNED

women who filled their pockets with stones,
then walked into the deepening pool
when the light was already grey, the air thick
with autumn grief, their bodies cool
in the slick rain, blue hands reaching upward
through waves, descending one step at a time.
For the men swept from their ships fully clothed,
their last words pinned close to their breasts,
the wind sucking in. The night is always pulling
on their sheets, running the dark space between hold
and release. Breathing deep. Their lungs full
of iron words. Pressing down. Lifting up. Listen
to their salt-swollen eyes: *The stars are heavy.*
So heavy. Carry me. Carry me home.
For the children down by the wide river bank,
still smelling of reeds and mud. Their mouths
hollow and still, caught mid-cry. No geese above.
No sound below. Their hair drying in the wind
after the storm. Beneath the clouds, the first birds return.
Leaves fill pockets and hands. For so many others who slip
down into graves too deep for hands or rope. Only light,
its thin and fragile line finds them now. Only the slow-eyed fish
counting bones. Even you, with hair the color of ink and stone,
are growing pale against the lake. The moon is a ripple above.
There are trees everywhere, their long dark arms just beyond reach.

THE MEMORY THEATRE

He calls this theatre of his by many names, saying now
that it is a built or constructed mind and soul,
and now that it is a windowed one.
        — Viglius writing to Erasmus
            on Guillo Camillo's Memory Theatre

A matter of wood, these many boxes,
icons, images, the assembly of which
boggles the mind. Or at least, replicates
a state of wonder. Though the man,
stammering in Latin to Erasmus'
correspondent, claims the pen has claimed
his tongue, rendered him speechless.

Now the two of them, in the dark space
between knowledge and completion,
consider wooden gangways. Seven.
Something about wisdom. One lane
larger than the others. Will there be mirrors?
The body is its own sign. The eye is an oracle.
Clay vessels rest in the corner. The doors
swing soundlessly without hinges.

In the balconies, old men are playing chess.
Crows gather at the gates. Shadows glisten
like blackened silver coins pulled from the gutter.
A trick of surfaces. Pits. Counterfeit.
The all-too-perfect gleam of teeth in winter.

WATER EPIGRAPH

What the other person said in passing
on this page or another,
in some dry-fingered book
taken down from the shelves,

or overheard in a stairwell
from two flights above,
in a cascade of dust, some apology
or acceptance — or a brief nirvana,
what birds hold in with their breath.

In the margins, this crowd
of shadow and ink, now
a matter of disagreement,
a token of worship, this fetish
we feed on.

Tables and the spiral of elements
laid out with the silverware,

the words he misspoke
at the party, turning one way,
while she went another

the dead do nothing for me

as if, sometimes he meant it,
or thought little of the seven
wonders of sorrow.

The four corners of his world
folding neatly in a pattern of absence
she could not resist.

She was all skin
on the bathroom floor
dreaming of blood.

Sorry, she said to the darkening blue
deepening around the drain.
        Sorry we can't go on.

THE MORTICIAN'S BOOKKEEPER

You arrive early to work,
clothed in a careful black
which you peel off layer by layer,
till white-sleeved and tieless
you descend into the stacks,
crunch numbers until the sun
slips out through the back door.

When things are slow, you too
might slip into a crowd of strangers,
fill an otherwise empty room,
or watch a casket burn in the brick oven.
Sometimes you help the dead dress,
comb back a loose hair, close an eye,
add color to their drying lips.

Some are so light, you could lift them
with a hand placed under the neck,
another arm stretched out to gather
the body at the knees, and walk
like a mother with a sleepless child
in a slow circle by the window light,
or the way a man with calloused hands
might carry his new bride up a long dark flight of stairs.

FOR SAL PARADISE, LOST IN AMERICA

I could drive for days on end
heading nowhere but out of the city,
out into a world of stone and wood,
plow and rain, and some cast-iron weather vane
spinning me whichever way the wind blows.

Go it alone
save only the static hum of the wheel-rutted roads
and the heart-ticking balm of silence.

A cradle of words, candle, camera,
and pen. Paper for fires. An arrow of stars.
A bow of earth yearning.

Tonight, I could be anywhere,
a lone man in a car surrounded by ghosts.

Outside my window, men and women
and the dark cloud of America

like a house burning
on a distant hill

I could be anywhere,

scattering over the world

I tell myself
how easy it would be

to be lost in the middle of America,
to be struck deaf, dumb, and blind by this star-splattered sky
and not know how to find my way home.

MAN PULLED FROM THE EARTH (EL SALVADOR)

for Sergio Moreno

A man who was pulled out alive 31 hours after the earthquake, and had come to symbolize hope to a country that has so little, died Tuesday night at a hospital.

— Associated Press

1.
How did they find your heartbeat
in so much silence?

Did they search the cracks in pavement tombs
after the earth finished trembling,
or was she still beating her breast in grief
when they broke through?

Did they find you sleeping, faint, or broken
beneath the weight of other's homes?

2.
You speak of the long-whiskered rats.
All night it seemed as if they prayed with you,
and for you recited litanies, prepared your soul
for its last movement, broke the silence
into small pieces. They covered your eyes
when you did not wish to sleep
but longed to break free,
a Lazarus in rags. Smelling of death,
you came forth from the dark worlds
still speaking in tongues.

3.

You did not remember your name, at first.
Such things were burdensome below,
too heavy for minds
preoccupied with breathing.
Choosing air over soil,
you filtered out dust with your lungs.
You concentrated on simple verbs
to be, to live, to go
into silence or into darkness.
It was a matter of maintaining the present tense
at all costs.
Breathe in. Breathe out.
Press body into clay
to seal wounds.
Wait for random ray of light
to find its way down
to skin,
to feel warm again
for a moment.

4.
When they pulled you from the earth
you did not speak.

Now, you ask hard questions
to an empty room,
wonder where your children lie.
How many times a man can return home alone
before the path becomes too worn,
what does the stone hear before it breaks?

You ask,
Is there a dream that does not end with the dreamer?

You do not know, but your arms have grown heavy
from holding on, so you let go,
watch your heart skim the torn earth
counting backwards through dreams
before you awake
                      again
                              and again.

IV

IN THE COUNTRY I CALL HOME

I have two countries, Cuba and the night.
— José Marti

There is no Cuba, no other half of night.
No dark woman in her deep robe of grief,
no wooden doors flung open to emptiness. Nothing
of music. No city in flames. All this absent.

In me, there are as many countries as names.
As many versions of the world.

If there is a country, it is a white-limbed tree,
a wind-drifted plain of snow. It is a country buried.
Or a man holding a camera to his eye. Or a silence.

If there is a country, there are two countries.
A double exposure. The other world ghosting the first.
The second full of dark-haired strangers. Ink ground
from charcoal pressed to stone. Hard as raw rice.

If there are two countries, a third always rises.
Life preserver on the waves. A ship without reference.
Anywhere. Everywhere. A nation of one.

If there are three, there must be a fourth.
I will find it in your skin. Hear it resonate in your bones.
A ringing echo. Something of sound. It will be small.
Almost a hut. A thatched roof shack in the wilderness.
A hermitage for two. A boat in a river. Almost a home.

HOW THE WORLD FITS TOGETHER

At best awkwardly, like new stones
in an old wall mended by strangers,
or the way the dead descend into the earth,
drifting like lost teeth in a broken jaw,
nothing certain of place.

Each fragment of world, a memory carried
across the dark soliloquy of water. What passes
beneath us and above, the sound of clouds,
the character of fire, the slow ease of hammers.

Draw me a schematic. A simple diagram of saints.
A symbolic representation of the world. *Dig here.*
Cross where it is shallow. *Here is a silence.*
Here is a moment. Here is a road.

Blackberry and reed. Salt water bridge of sand.
Iron girder story. False mercy of flame. Outside,
the gun bone rattle of children at war. A bus burning
like a candle. Flickering wax statue of peace.

Carry me home in barbed wire tangles. Lips of obsidian.
Eyes like coal. Skeleton of bark. Dream beneath rivers.
The dying — the unyielding curvature of light and longing.
The moon's dark mane of cloud trailing and falling
till we wake at last, watching — uncertain,

our hands merging, folding one into the other
like an echo of storms carried in a hundred paper boats
or the endless chain of names which wed the sky
to the world below. Here, any god could be my god.
The earth. The coin. This bitter map of numbers
I taste on your tongue.

AFTER NERUDA

Suddenly, everything is a woman.

The way a street lamp curves
at the edge of a dark lane,
or an orchid blooms in an empty room,
patient for destruction, beautiful as a white slip
floating in the wrecking ball's wake.

You hear the sea in everything,
its great bell-like waves sounding
deep in your anxious sleep, moving invisibly
by your ears with each passing car.

Light takes on a strange quality,
like the once-familiar scent of women
you have known or the texture of old bus tokens,
worn smooth in pockets, no longer in currency.

You want to make love
in a language you do not know,
or write prayers between the lines
of old dollar bills given to strangers.

You caress the backs of pews,
pray to unknown gods you have witnessed
from your window, their half-closed eyes
flashing in the distance, like lighthouses in a storm.

In the kitchen, you surround yourself
with apples, lemons, and a tomato.
Arranging them in silence, you can sense
her presence just beneath the skin.

When you hold the tomato to your ear
you can hear her breathing in ragged sighs,
like a ship heaving against the tide.

When you press it to your lips,
you can still taste the unwashed salt of sorrow.

WHAT I KNOW ABOUT ABSTRACTION

The moon is made of hammered tin. And tonight, Sorrow
must be the bone grey sparrow I found lying in the fields
east of the freeway: one wing broken, one eye the color
of rusted steel. And by it, eager for flight, a white paper cup
wrestling with the evening wind.

Down at the water's edge, I know nothing of the two men rowing.
All night they skirt the shore, the bridge, the abandoned docks.
The same shadows returning till I think they are twins
in their dark raincoats, their eyes a blur. One pulls an antique bottle
from his sleeve, which might be Hope,

and throws it as far as he can into the deep, then lies back
and sighs, as if to say, *There is nothing more that can be offered
to the world tonight.* Will it float? Will it sink? Who knows?
Tomorrow, I might see it grace the gravel beach, shattered
by the waves, or whole. Something inevitably returns with the tide.

Something like the cup now flying in the wind, a white glow
in the dark which could be Truth or any star before it fades
behind clouds or is lost beyond the stand of sycamores where Love
is no doubt digging ditches row after row, building a cemetery
at the edge of the world.

I am certain of this, leaning against the rail on a hill
that oversees this town, where Memory might be last year's bicycle
painted red, the tires losing air with each turn. And the girl
on the corner in the borrowed dress is Sleep, the one
the last drunk will carry home in his arms before dawn.

THE CENTER OF MEMORY

Someone called it *hippocampus*, meaning "seahorse,"
what it resembled when the skull was opened
to an arbitrary page, the dull grey text of the brain
almost unreadable in the absent light. Did they say it,
thinking of a man on a horse moving through the river
of forgetting, waist deep and dreaming? Was he trailing a net?
Was he scanning the waves for what remains of a day?
These bicycle frames. Gull feathers. Down from old pillows.
Your arms spread open like a bird in flight, poised
on the parking tower ledge over the city. The sun,
curved around corners, stretching the trees.
Or even the shadows of glass towers and windows.
The way light bends through water. Sound is different
in the ears of a drowning man. Garbled.
Or Garbo, with her hypnotic gaze. Husky voice.
Face registering everything or nothing. A certain
synesthesia which leads me to believe in the color *nine*,
or the deepest sound of *red*.

ELEGY FOR GREY

Not quite cloud or brine, the color
of drifting ash, or a birch's thin pale
at twilight. This aftermath of fire.
Half-toned sleep of the closing eye
of the dead. A potter's hand full
of watery clay. Slip. What fills the cracks
in old brick walls and ships, beneath
the greening moss. Fossil color of bone.

Mother-of-pearl. What lurks behind
faded ink. Newspapers shedding
their skins. The wings of egrets poised
at the water's edge. Wind over graves.
Snow at dusk. The water's film running
backward. To sorrow. To lament.
Vesuvius dreaming. Gravel roads
turning northward. The soft gleam
of unearthed pearl or hair.

What the waves return. Sorrow.
Driftwood. Worn tires. Bits of chrome.
Weathered imprecision of photographs found
beneath squirrels flickering in the dark-limbed trees.
From the shadows, birds call
unnamed. Unknown, like a man
pointing through fog to the sound of oars,
or the unseen shudder of gulls.
Distance. The light failing.
A suitcase in the rain.

What we do not say
at the close of night.

TRAVELING THROUGH THE PRAIRIES,
I THINK OF MY FATHER'S VOICE

How we must have seemed like twins over the phone,
my father speaking with my voice, I speaking with his.
Some strange accident of genetics or the unchecked influence

of mockingbirds and mimeographs. I have heard two trains sound
almost alike till they passed, like the one last night bending westward,
the other slowing to a halt, the earth shuddering in the dark between,

while the stars held their place overhead, a thousand points of tin and fire.
Had it been day, I might have seen to the far faded edge of nowhere
or whatever town lies wakeless there. Here, the wind sounds the same

blown from any direction, full of dust, pollen, the deep toll of church bells
rung for mass, weddings, deaths. Coming through on the straight road,
the land seems especially bare this year, although the fields are still green

with new stalks of wheat, rye, canola. Someone has been taking down
the grain elevators one by one, striking their weathered wooden frames
from the skyline, leaving only small metal bins. The way the disease

took him by degrees, the body jettisoning what it could: his arms and legs,
his grin, his laugh, his voice. In the end, only his eyes — their steel doors
opening and closing while the storm rattled within — and his breath,

the body's voice, repeating the only name it knew sigh after sigh,
a lullaby sung to a restless child on a heaving deck, a hush we only learn
in the quiet dark long after the boat has gone and the waves have ceased.

KITE FLYING

Late summer, when the winds blew hard,
I would blend into the sand, while my father stood
at the edge of the beach watching the kite rise
against the dark pines, and the line which tethered it
to his hands, became invisible in the half-light of dusk.

How it pulled heavenward into the insubstantial blue,
or circled twisting in the breeze, falling then rising again,
always beyond reach. And he would stand gesturing,
as if calling a stray dog home or a cat from a tree. A secret spell,
something only he knew to waken the creature in the sky,
to send it running out to sea like an angry pike on a line, then return
exhausted to his hand. And when winds struck, it could seem
as if the whole kite would burst with longing to leave the earth.

What an old song this is — what flies above our heads
like a banner, a wish for the one who never comes home.

CREDO

Not so much the world, but what it signifies:
last year's rain still sleeping in the deepest wells,
or the cherry trees arched over stone walls. Yearning.
The earth bent around a weathered pine. Old stoves
tipped and sleeping, iron rusting into green. Forgetting.
God is always in the places I cannot reach, be He blackbird
or raven. Even the geese guillotining the sky mean something
to the girl laid down in the weeds. Someone is speaking in darkness,
a voice like sorrow, something like tin, the sun, even in sin, even then, I
believe. All night, our prayers rise like dust. Our voices reach
like seed for rain.

KUNDIMAN

This morning, the sun not yet piercing the grey Virginia world,
I wake already with longing for those I soon will leave —
whose voices, raw and importuning, have peeled away
my skin and laid open my chest with the finest of cuts.
Here, in the space enclosed by the white bones of my ribs,
a heart beats with the wonder of so many tongues — no,
it moves like a ship on this dark ocean of home and departure.
Each of us rowing, beat after beat, page after page, haunted by words.
Speak again of salt, lovers lost, of the body muted, of our fathers,
mothers, brothers, sisters, daughters, sons. You who knock at the wooden
door of a guitar at midnight. You who let words carry your limbs
and lips. You who rumble deep into sorrow or anger or unrequited joy.
Tell me now, who will lift us when we are weary? Who will fill us
with the dark beauty of song? What will we say tomorrow,
when we rise to take our next train, next bus, next taxi, or plane? When we
return to the cities we have loved or despised for so long?
What will we say to the open door, to the room full of now?

THE ART OF MEMORY

for Simonides of Ceos

All memory is a matter of place,
the ordered setting of the world
and how we walk through it.
Our eyes trained to perceive meaning
or congruence with lines from old plays,
speeches we did not deliver, the names
of beetles, the parts of a fish laid open
by a blade. Even the guests crushed
beneath the tiles of a fallen hall
in ancient Greece can be recalled,
table by table. Their loud voices dimmed
to a silence.

Do not rely on columns or statues.
The constellations will do. Each
darkened house rimmed with light,
and the yawning curve of the earth
and sea. Choose natural signs.
The dead for the dead. A man holding
a quill. A ram with blood-tipped horns.
Paper folded in squares, glowing in fire.
Even my father, walking the rooms
of the old house before it is sold,
fixing in his mind the colors of the walls,
the hallways and doors, the last traces
of home before we break free.

MY FATHER, WAKING TO WORK

after Robert Hayden

Early mornings, my father would rise
to the house still cold, the windows'
fine print of frost, and dress in the dark.
Always the creak of boards, the stairs
tread down, then the door pressed closed.
Firm. The solid click of the bolt, then off
into the first grey of dawn. The black ice
roads. From my upper window, the shadows
of wartime homes would fall away.
His car now only an anonymous fog.
How the trees were bared. The fences almost
forgotten by light. The faint gleam of red
before his turn beyond the hill. And always
something lingered. The damp smell of boots.
Books in their thousands. The aisles
in that warehouse that could have been a home.

FIRST POEM

I cannot recall what I wrote, except
that predictably it was for a girl. Dark-haired
or blond, the time-dimmed details escape me.
Even her name.

         But I am certain it was fall,
when we dug out our winter coats
from the dark memories of closets,
ready by the door for a brighter world
that bit sharply at our cheeks.

And I think that her skin grew whiter
every day, at least it seems so now.
Her eyes were still and distant, two strangers
who had packed their bags all night, and now
stood wordless at a window, the gravel shore below,
waves rolling in, one after another.

And when she was gone into the earth, and the teacher came
to speak of blood and bones and death, and how to grieve,
and how to live, I left no flowers on her empty seat,
carried no cards. Went home instead, and wrote some lines
and her name to hide in a box beneath my bed,
now lost somewhere, beyond recall.

AN HOUR BEFORE ARRIVING, I SEE HOME

The fields scraped clean with frost
and the city's haze, barely visible ahead.
To the side, wells quiet with the iron taste
of water. The road, the earth's thin seam,
a straight cut through this body of unseen grain.
What is closest is still. What is merciless
is newly grown on the dark panes
of abandoned farm houses. Everything
winds upward, even the world pressed flat
like the last edge of the hour, and this hand
turning round and round and round.

THE SHAPE OF THINGS

Nothing about us that we can see is permanent.
Or so it seems, now that the great walls are gone,
save only a few remnants of the ones the Romans
raised with stone and mortar.
                    What the wind does not take away,
it conceals behind a magician's screen. All fire
and mirrors. The blackening sky and the strained length
of cloud, mere echoes of last year's lines carved
by the farmer with his plow. The black dress hung
in the rafters could easily fade and mingle with dust,
but something of its shadow remains. How loss
clings to a shape, how it loves a form. Like water,
or the late summer rain which cannot halt the last leaf's fall,
but blesses the oak nonetheless, a consolation of sorts,
a farewell the color of lightning and flame. Whatever it is —
that having filled its measure, must ultimately overflow.

PRODIGAL

Here is a grief grown white as the moon tonight,
so round with yearning
                    your mother has no more words.

She will not say she has come alone to the shore again
to draw something from the dark echo of waves —

some memory of you as a boy with impossibly small hands.
You with hair that will not part. You curled in the space
between bodies like a small bulb of light.

Not how you left, so awkward and pained,
your want as deep as the fear in your knees,
as the regret in the hollowed bones beneath your skin

or that betraying hand, the one that trembled at your side
by the last needle wound. Your eyes now as still as pebbles
laid in the river bed with no memory of mountains or shores.

She cannot say hell, cannot whisper God
or even the grave and its diligent worms. What is belief then?
What is faith? If she lets these go, what then?

We want what we cannot see, the other face of the moon,
the one missing. The one turned away at this precise moment.

We want to see, but it is dark in here, in this small narrow world.
It is dark always, then someone opens a door.
Then another. Then another.

There are more rooms than two in the world beyond.
Somewhere her son is sleeping.

I DREAM MY FATHER ON THE SHORE

What I am learning to give you is my death.
— Wendell Berry

Outside, beneath the light of late October's candled sky
the weave of ash and maple burns. We stand silent on the graveled shore.
My father lifts his father's ashes from its urn, a strangely heavy thing,
he seems to say, his arms swaying, then casting out into the long dark
as if to throw a line, while we wait for some sound, a wave,
whatever marks the distance between a father and a son.

And when night comes, it comes without a tread, without a word.
The stars, flickering in their endless retreat, more distant and sure
than before, do nothing while the shadows continue to fill the trees
with their cast-off clothes. The harvest is long past, the apples
have fallen to the orchard floors. Even my father turning to go
is almost lost to the reeds already in his path, his figure no more
than a pattern of light — a memory of a road that winds
through the darkness to our waiting ride home.

NOTES

"Outside Plato's Republic, the Last Poets Wait for Departure" was inspired by the experiences of the poets who left China in the aftermath of the 1989 Tiananmen Square Massacre. The epigraph is taken from "On the Poet, Poetry, and Poetics," a short article by Liu Hongbin, one of those who chose exile over imprisonment. The title alludes to Plato's exclusion of poets from his vision of the ideal society.

"To Jeremiah, Dreaming" is addressed to the Old Testament prophet, Jeremiah, who spent much of his life in prison in Jerusalem.

"Litany" was inspired by the angel poems of Rafael Alberti.

The river of lamps in the last lines of "Here and There" refers to tōrō nagashi, a Japanese ceremony on the last night of the Obon festival, where paper lanterns are floated down a river to guide the spirits of the departed back to the other world. Joshua Tree is Joshua Tree National Park, California. This poem is dedicated to the memory of Nancy Lambert.

"The Memory Theatre" is based on an account of the physical structure invented by Giulio Camillo Delminio (1480-1544) , which combined classical memory systems with Renaissance occult patterns and images. An excellent description of the nature and complexity of the Theatre can be found in Frances A. Yates' *The Art of Memory* (University of Chicago Press, 1966, pp. 129-159). The epigraph is drawn from correspondence between Vigilius and Erasmus (Erasmus, *Epistoplae*, ed. P.S. Allen & others, IX, p. 479)

"For Sal Paradise, Lost in America" is addressed to the protagonist of Jack Kerouac's *On the Road*.

"In the Country I Call Home" responds to José Marti's poem, "Two Countries." The epigraph comes from the first line of the same poem.

"Kundiman" refers both to a type of traditional Filipino folk song of unrequited love, which often doubled as a veiled expression of patriotism in times of colonial occupation, and to the Asian American writing organization and retreat by the same name.

"The Art of Memory" is dedicated to Simonides of Ceos, the Greek poet credited by Cicero as being the father of memory and memory systems. The story goes that Simonides was once invited to perform at a large indoor banquet hall. Having received word of a messenger awaiting him, he had stepped out only to have the building collapse behind him killing all the guests. When the families despaired that there would be no way to determine who had been killed, Simonides responded that he could recall each table's occupants from memory having memorized them earlier by their places at each table.

"My Father, Waking to Work" was inspired by Robert Hayden's "Those Winter Sundays."

"Prodigal" is for Heather L.

The epigraph for "I Dream My Father on the Shore" comes from a line in Wendell Berry's poem, "The Country of Marriage."

ABOUT THE AUTHOR

Neil Aitken was born in Vancouver, British Columbia and grew up in Saudi Arabia, Taiwan, and various parts of western Canada and the United States. He worked for a number of years as a computer games programmer before leaving the industry in 2004 to complete an MFA at the University of California, Riverside. He is currently pursuing a PhD in literature and creative writing at the University of Southern California.

His poems have appeared in *Barn Owl Review, Crab Orchard Review, The Drunken Boat, Poetry Southeast, RHINO, Sou'wester,* and *Washington Square,* as well as in the anthologies *Blue Arc West: An Anthology of California Poets* and *Homage to Vallejo.* He is the founding editor of *Boxcar Poetry Review,* a Kundiman fellow, and three-time Pushcart Prize nominee. *The Lost Country of Sight* is his first book.